33 WAYS TO GET MOTIVATED & STAY IN THE ZONE

WALTER PATRICK, JR.

www.walterpatrickjr.com

33 Ways to Get Motivated & Stay in the Zone/ Walter Patrick, Jr. —1st ed.
ISBN 9781731330000

CONTENTS

ACKNOWLEDGMENTS

To my son Brenden. You have taught me more than you can ever imagine. Your drive, patience, and exquisiteness to believe in the process are infectious, not only to me, but also to those you have encountered and associated with. Many have told you, even encouraged you, to change your dream and pursue something more secure, but you stayed true to yourself, motivated, spent quality time with God, and have prepared yourself immensely for the many opportunities that will continuously be presented to you. You are my hero.

To my best friend Susan, with gratitude and praise, I thank you for your support, belief, and confidence in me even when acrimonious statements were being made. We are best friends forever!

To my sister Yvette, who has demonstrated to me what happiness is even when times are tough. My love and feelings for you will always be unconditional and magnified by the days.

To my friend Dwight, I cannot thank you enough for your genuine support in many different areas of my life. You have encouraged me to be strong even in the midst of the storms, because it cannot rain forever.

And to Brunella Costagliola, Jonathan Agin, JuLee Brand, Erin McKnight and the team at Kevin Anderson & Associates for your editing services and helping me publish my first book.

MY STORY

I am a public speaker, entrepreneur, and medical sales consultant who resides in Livermore, California. I have earned an MBA and a BS (aeronautical engineering)/MS from Cal Poly San Luis Obispo. I also hold a real estate broker license and have been the recipient of many medical sales awards. I have owned several businesses, all achieved without a high school diploma, GED, and/or middle school education. When most seventh graders were in school, I was hitchhiking from the west coast (Berkeley, California) to the east coast (Daytona Beach, Florida), and oftentimes working at traveling carnivals to survive in the early 70s. I was born in Daytona Beach, Florida, and, by the time I was four, my dad had moved my younger sister and me to Oakland, California, to pursue his education. One year later my mother moved from Florida to California to live with my dad, sister, and myself. After one year my mother and dad split up and she took my sister and me back to Sanford, Florida, to live with her and her parents only to find out my mother's parents did not want her and two kids living with them so my mother dropped my sister and me off at our dad's parents' house in Daytona Beach, Florida, because we were not welcome in my mom's mother and father's house in Sanford, Florida. Coincidently our dad's older brother had just been discharged from the military and he drove my sister (one year old) and myself (five years old) from Daytona Beach, Florida, back to Oakland, California, where my dad was living with his sister because he was out of work. By the grace of God, I graduated from elementary school, after being in and out of juvenile hall, detention centers, group homes, foster homes, friends' homes, family members' homes, and pretty much anywhere else I could find shelter. After running away from a boarding home in San Francisco at the age of 14, I carpooled from San Francisco to Berkeley and hitched from Berkeley, California, back to Daytona Beach, Florida, to my grandparents' home intuitively searching for my self-identity and purpose in life. I knew deep down inside of me there was more to life than the cards I had been dealt thus far. I arrived in Daytona Beach, Florida, on a Friday after several weeks of hitchhiking and working at carnivals to save money. My grandfather picked me up from the Florida airport and took me to his house where I was greeted with love, admiration, and lots of questions from my grandmother. My grandparents were in disbelief that a child of my age could actually hitchhike from California to Florida at such a young age. My grandmother had throat cancer with a hole in the middle of her neck so her words were raspy but I remember her saying, "I love you but I have to send you back to your dad." I was devastated about returning back to California, especially after the long nights of sleeping outside and in trucks to make it to Daytona Beach, Florida. There was a little comfort in knowing I would not have to hitchhike back to California. I spent Saturday morning explaining to my grandparents the various stops I made with the carnival, my responsibility of setting up the roller coaster ride, and the many stops I made while hitchhiking and the variety of people I met. My grandmother washed my clothes Saturday afternoon and hung them outside to dry. She took me to church on Sunday morning and put me on a Greyhound bus Sunday evening with a bucket of chicken heading back to California where I knew I was in serious trouble because I was supposed to be at a boarding home in San Francisco.

I had experienced some incredibly hard times by the age of 12, such as sleeping outside behind bushes for several weeks after running away from home. I would often hear my dad walking to the bus stop early in the morning on his way to work as I was hiding behind the bushes I had slept behind the night before; oftentimes it was very cold. As a 12-year-old I was terrified that my dad may see me in the bushes and begin beating me so I was very still and quiet as he passed by. My dad had a set routine in order for him to catch the bus to work. I knew what time he would be walking by because I could hear his footsteps as he got closer, but the brush was just dense enough to keep me hidden and out of sight. After he had passed by I would sneak back to the house, which was six blocks away, after everyone had left for school and work. I would break in through the back door and get something to eat before anyone would return home. Once the fall and winter came I had to find different sleeping arrangements because of the cold and rainy weather so I started sleeping in Greyhound buses parked at the Greyhound bus stations in downtown Oakland, California. During those days, Trailways bus doors were always locked but Greyhound bus doors were left unlocked, and I would take shelter inside of the bus to stay warm and out of the bushes. When the bus doors were locked I would rent a room at the YMCA, which was two blocks away from the Greyhound bus station, and when I didn't have the cash for a room I would stay at a homeless shelter (because I didn't feel welcome at home) all between the ages of 12, 13, and 14, which is the timeframe I was sent to foster homes, group homes, camps, detention centers, and juvenile hall. I often asked myself what I did to deserve this type of punishment and humiliation because it did not seem to match any mischievous conduct I could have been participating in. As a child I experienced some of the worst beatings from my parents, anything from wire pliers pinching the fingers to water hose beatings to being tied up and then beaten; the list goes on. I have memories of being chained to trees in the backyard while the family went on outings, tied up and beaten in the basement to standing on one foot for more than 24 hours, and, if my foot accidentally touched the floor, that would be additional punishment right on the spot. I recall as a kid going to the Oakland police department, to have pictures taken of my entire body. Someone must have informed my parents if they were to continue beating me in this manner they would be charged with child abuse, because the beating ceased. God's intervention is the main reason I'm alive today, and not completely bruised from head to toes.

I share this not to say my parents were horrible people who enjoy punishing and beating me but to illustrate the power of God and how He has protected his children. You will inevitably experience adversity from those people who should be fueling you with love and encouragement. Be careful with who you closely associate with; there will be family, friends, acquaintances, and associates, be sure you know the difference. You should be responsible for your destiny, not anyone else, because when you are discovering your why in life and on a path to success there will be those that are questioning your ability and/or discouraging you from accomplishing your goals. When determining your why you are here, be strong like ants, who will find a way to accomplish their tasks no matter how many obstacles are placed in their way. The ants will die trying to go over, around, or through their obstacle.

Some may argue my parents were abusive, but there is one thing I've learned from my dad that has carried me through life and still does. While playing strikeout on an elementary school playground in Oakland, California (Manzanita elementary) with the box and strike zone written with chalk on the back wall, he was throwing the tennis ball with an enormous amount of velocity aiming for the strike zone and he said "never give up." To this day I am not sure if my dad realized the enormous effect of his words but as a kid I inherently started applying that concept and made it my mantra: "never give up." I added a little more to it once I started attending college, which was "It may take you a little longer but never give up." It did take me a little longer to graduate from college but I never gave up. When you don't give up, you will win most of the time because most people will give up under pressure and not even attempt to reach their true potential.

Even though I had no formal education, I was able to land my first job as a bellman at 16 years old at the Leamington Hotel in downtown

Oakland, California, where some of the greatest performers lodged before and after their performances at the Paramount Theatre, which was around the corner. I landed the job by knowing how to spell my name and using my parents' address for my residences on the application although I was not living there. This job has proved to be incredibly important for a couple of reasons: 1) I was still living on my own with no income or support and 2) I ended up making a career in the hospitality industry and working as a night auditor to pay my way through college. In the process of working 37 different jobs, attending five different junior colleges, being evicted three times, car repossessed twice, and denied financial aid twice, I managed to finally graduate from Merritt Junior College in 1986 at the age of 24 with an associate's degree in science and heading to Cal Poly San Luis Obispo with a declared major in aeronautical engineering.

I still remember my math instructor at Merritt Junior College telling me after class one day I should apply at Cal Poly, because I was pretty good at math. I was extremely good at math, mainly because I was a night auditor, which consists of lots of portfolio reconciliations during the swing shift (11 p.m.-7 a.m.). Going to school from 8 a.m.-2 p.m. and sleeping from 3 p.m.-9 p.m. was tough some days, especially since the sun was still up as I was going to bed. It took me over seven years to get a two-year degree but it was worth it. Once the math instructor told me I should reach out to Cal Poly I contacted the counselor at Cal Poly to ask about that admission process that same day and the consular immediately asked me what major I was interested in. I replied, "What is your toughest major?" The counselor replied, "Aeronautical engineering." I declared my major in aeronautical engineering right on the spot. After everything I had gone through, the intensity of this major surely didn't scare me enough to back away from it; I looked at this major as just another challenge.

Fast-forwarding to the week of college orientation, at one of the ceremonial speeches, the president of the engineering department asked all the students to stand up and hold hands. He then said, "Look at the person on your left, now look at the person on your right. I have been president at Cal Poly for 20 years and the persons you just looked at, they will not graduate from Cal Poly SLO." I was in the aeronautical engineering department and holding hands with two wealthy Caucasian guys who didn't have to work while attending college or before going to college, they had performed very well on the SAT, which I never took or the GED. They looked at me with a look as if I had been defeated before the first day of class started. Although I did not possess all the accolades, background, and/or pedigree as my peers at the time, I still felt I could compete academically with the best. My belief was and still is, with the right motivation and a little time, beating the odds was and is just a matter of time. When not writing, I enjoy reading, exercising, snowboarding, and golfing.

Believe in God. Build yourself up. Have standards that you won't go below. That way you can come into all your relationships from a position of strength.
Bishop T.D. Jakes

INTRODUCTION

In a fast-paced culture seeking immediate results, we must learn the exquisiteness of patience, effort, and perseverance (PEP). Be strong in your mind, present in your spirit, and steadfast in your efforts. Have you ever come up with an idea or concept and talked yourself out of moving forward with it, but then, later in life, you saw or heard about someone else implementing your idea with great success?

The only difference between you, Jack Dorsey (Twitter), Mark Zuckerberg (Facebook), and Evan Spiegel (Snapchat) is that they came up with an idea, identified resources to help with implementation, and were inspired and motivated to never give up. Moving fast and having a sense of urgency is the one thing you can develop that will separate you from everyone else. You should develop a bias for action. When you get a good idea, move forward with it. The faster you move forward with your idea, the better you'll get at handling adversity; the better you get at handling adversity, the more you'll like yourself; the more you like yourself, the higher your self-esteem; the higher your self-esteem, the greater your self-discipline; the greater your self-discipline, the more you will become persistent at achieving your goals, and then you will ultimately become unstoppable with implementing your thoughts and ideas.

It has been said that the richest place in the world is the graveyard; that's because most great ideas die due to the inability of individuals getting motivated enough to execute on them. We often tell ourselves we're going to make something happen, we're going to get it done this time. Yet, nothing happens. That's because we didn't follow through, as we didn't have the right rituals in place. Rituals are the little things we do each day to build us up gradually, condition our body, our mind, and our soul to make things happen. I will explain how to carry through an idea to its conclusion, no matter how meager. Your rituals, self-talk, goal-setting, and prioritizing will motivate you daily. I have learned, and would like to share with you, how implementing these skills can be the catalyst to achieving your maximum performance consistently. In my book 33 Ways to Get Motivated & Stay in the Zone, I will provide important keys to unlock your potential energy and convert it into kinetic energy. What makes this book different is its ability to explain complex ideas and science-backed strategies in a simple, accessible way that you can implement every day.

Motivation is based on two primary principles and reasonably exact science: causes and effects through individual rituals and self-talk have been analyzed and are well understood. This book reveals how to identify rituals and take action to ensure they are positively charged to yield the maximum benefits for you. We know what is most effective, and we often act on basic law, which is to follow the path of least resistance, unless motivated to move out from an illusionary comfort zone. Once you give your engine a jump, it becomes easier to keep it going; once you get a refrigerator moving on a dolly, it's easier to keep it moving; everything is easier once it's in motion. You don't have to be great to get started but you have to get started to be great.

Therefore, this book does not deal with theories and opinions, but with well-proved principles, concepts, facts, and personal experiences. It is a book for students and professionals (business leaders, owners, salespeople, customer service representatives, and human service professionals) who would like to accomplish their goals and fulfill their dreams. Every statement has been weighed. This book is established on fundamentals.

MOTIVATION

You don't have to be great to get started but
you have to get started to be great.
Unknown

Everyone always talks about "becoming motivated" and "staying motivated." But what is motivation and why is it so vital for success? Motivation is when you have an idea and carry it through to its conclusion not 70%, 80%, nor 90%, but all the way to 100%. Motivation is a state of the heart, mind, and soul that is continuously seeking out new opportunities, challenges, and finding out what you love to do while fulfilling your life with that. It's this passion, inner drive, and desire that keeps you going daily. Motivation is also the force that drives you to work hard; it's the catalyst to action. Motivation is simply a function of goal-setting and self-regulation (self-monitoring), and it is mathematically expressed as:

$$Motivation = Goal\text{-}setting + Self\text{-}regulation$$

This approach allows you to compare your self-performance to your goals, which will yield either self-satisfaction or dissatisfaction and, based on this principle, you will either move towards your goals, stall, or abandon them altogether. Motivation, along with inspiration, is required to accomplish anything in life; without it, nothing would ever get done. I don't want this to sound contrary to common sense, but consider the alternative: without motivation and inspiration there would not be any desire or eagerness to get stuff done. Motivation is comprised of two primary elements:

A)   Intensity of behavior or arousal

B)   Direction of behavior

Studies have proven that the level of arousal is directly correlated to an individual's performance and, slightly above arousal, is when individuals tend to reach pinnacle performances. Hence, arousal can be defined as a general state of activation or excitement ranging from deep sleep to extreme excitement. Individuals manifest or experience stress differently, and the level of arousal has a direct correlation to one's performance. The first element of motivation can be explained using the Drive Theory.

The Drive Theory is the relationship between arousal and performance. Increased arousal increases the probability of your dominant response to occur. If your talent is simple or well-rehearsed, such as a basketball player practicing free throws, then heightened arousal will enhance their performance. If arousal is high, you will tend to go to what is most comfortable or habitual for you; hopefully, what is comfortable is what you should be doing. The second element is the direction of the behavior: you should find out if you are motivated to move towards things (rewards) or move away from them. Generally when things get rewarded, they get done and when things are not rewarded, the desire to accomplish the task decreases substantially.

TYPES OF MOTIVATION

Even if you are on the right track, you will get run over if you just sit there.
Will Rogers

The first type of motivation is intrinsic motivation, which is what motivates your instincts; for example, if you enjoy playing music, the intrinsic factor is the feeling you experience when notes are played correctly and you feel as though everything is in harmony, going well, and you receive gratification from your efforts. Another example is when a relationship is going well, and you are internally motivated to continue investing in this relationship, even though nobody is going to give you a medal for your effort.

"The great athletes are not motivated by money. You cannot get players like Montana, Craig, Lott, Rice, Young, and other players we have, and say they were strictly motivated by money. Their sense of pride, sense of duty, sense of theirs jobs, and future is and was very important. They are self-motivators," says former San Francisco 49ers' owner Eddie DeBartolo Jr. Intrinsic motivation seems to be the key. The intangible rewards for athletes, as well as yourself, should be more important than the monetary gains. It's all about striving to do your best.

With extrinsic motivation, individual participants receive plaques, medals, money, and sponsorship for their efforts in the activity they are participating in.

Human kinetic research shows that athletes who have the best motivational outcomes, such as persistence, efforts, positive attitude, and good pre-concentration, tend to be both extrinsically and intrinsically motivated. Athletes who are primarily extrinsically motivated tend to become discouraged when they do not perform up to expectations. For example, when I ran in my first marathon, I trained for a specific finishing time, and when the official results were posted and my goal was not achieved, I was discouraged and looked for excuses as to why my finishing time was way off the mark (no pacer and/or faulty watch not keeping accurate pacing and time). Conversely, there were people running in the marathon just to complete it, without a pacer and no specific finishing time goals, other than to finish the race running or walking.

Therefore, if you are predominantly intrinsically motivated, you often do not have that competitive drive to become a champion. This is because you tend to enjoy mastering the task that comprises the chosen discipline and it doesn't matter if it's running, playing an instrument, or opening a business. When you are predominantly intrinsically motivated, you lack the strong competitive streak.

In the long run, extrinsic motivation is only effective when intrinsic motivation is high. You need to practice the proper techniques to achieve your goal and make sure you are doing it for yourself and not for anyone else. What I mean here is, when you try to accomplish a task, make sure you get the details right and fall in love with the process of achieving your goals. Being driven solely by extrinsic motivation is fun and gratifying, but not psychologically healthy, because the lack of intrinsic rewards can lead to quitting or seriously questioning your involvement.

Intrinsic motivation helps you get through the dry and rough patches in your competitions, academics, and training, and keeps emphasis on having fun. If you are not marching towards your goals, you are doing something wrong, and you need to adjust your goals or approach, which is one of the reasons why professionals seek personal trainers and coaches to help them build good habits and rituals.

3.

RITUALS

Your habits are driving your performance.
Your rituals are creating your success.
Robin Sharma

Rituals define you, so much so that all the results we accomplish in our life derive from our rituals. If you're out of shape and overweight, for example, you have a different set of rituals than someone who is physically fit. If you're fit, chances are you're receiving the proper amount of rest, eating healthy, and you are exercising during the course of the week. If you're out of shape, you oversleep, have an unhealthy diet and do not exercise, or have a genetic predisposition. Each of our DNA and body metabolisms are different, therefore this may be a small bit of exaggeration but it's pretty much the norm for individuals in shape and out of shape. My biological alarm is set for 4:15 a.m. and I am in the gym by 4:50 a.m., with my bed made and ready to tackle one of my most challenging tasks first.

Failures occur in the same way. All your little daily failures come together and can cause you to have a failure of titanic proportions, just like all your little successes will eventually add up to large accomplishments. For example you might fail to get up on time, meaning you no longer had time to go the gym, the next day you may fail to send that e-mail that would have secured you that one client who was eager to work with you. Another day, you might fail to pay that vendor who, as a result, will no longer wish to work with you. And, before you know it, your business would have failed because you failed to take small, yet fundamental, steps to success.

When I was getting ready to run in my first marathon, I meticulously followed a rigid running schedule (to avoid any side effects or injuries), which would increase the probability of my success. Not only was I able to complete the marathon (Thanks, run Disney), but I also went shopping at an outdoor mall afterwards and walked an additional five miles. In life, you can't expect to suddenly become successful at something; success is paid for in advance. The secret is to work on a future goal a little bit at a time, but consistently, in order to achieve and be successful at it.

4.

DEVELOPING GOOD HABITS

Motivation gets you going and habit gets you there.
Zig Ziglar

Developing good habits is critical to getting motivated. Your body and mind should almost be on autopilot, especially in the morning (your morning doesn't have to be in the a.m., it could depend on your work schedule, if you work late your morning could start in the p.m.). You increase your probability of having a positive morning start by spending your first few hours doing things you have already preplanned. By having a morning routine you are starting your day with a plan and setting the tone for a productive day. Habits are essentially shortcuts that are meant to make you more efficient and motivated throughout the day. I once heard that former President Barack Obama only had two suit colors, blue and black, so he didn't have to waste time deciding on what color shirt to wear or what color suit to wear; it was either blue or black, keeping it simple and allowing him to allocate time to life's bigger challenges.

The key to creating good habits is to have a strategy, convert that strategy into a rule, and then convert the rule into a habit. Research has shown that it takes 21 days to create a habit for something simple, such as placing your keys and/or workout clothes the night before so that in the morning you won't have to waste time looking for them. However, for more complex tasks, it takes a little longer, on average 66 days to be exact. And how long it takes for this new habit to form will vary depending on the individual and the circumstances involved. In a study by health psychology researcher Phillippa Lally, it took anywhere from 18 days to 254 days for individuals to form a new habit.

Essentially, your day is comprised of three components:

1) **Appointments:** prior commitments you have made with someone else or yourself
2) **A to-do list:** a list of tasks that need to be completed
3) **Habits:** should be on autopilot, such as waking up at 4:15 a.m. and brushing your teeth

Appointments, your to-do list, and good habits will keep you motivated to complete tasks. Yes, you're going to have some slight modifications during the course of your day, but do not be alarmed. Make adjustments and continue moving forward. I remember watching Mo Farah, the Olympic marathon runner, fall in the middle of the race only to get back up and win the gold medal; he made the adjustment and continued moving forward towards his goal. Be sure you know why things changed and embrace change, because change is constant and inevitable. Change can be either positive or negative and by understanding how change is impacting you can help you better prepare for success. In the above incident with Mo Farah the Olympic runner, the runner in front of him slowed down and his change in speed created a cascading effect resulting in Mo Farah colliding with him and taking a fall. I was a day trader in the dot-com era and one day noticed my stock was losing value, but stayed optimistic the stock would bounce back the next day; it didn't and I lost a ton of money only to realize a few days later, the company I had invested in did not meet the market expectations. Had I taken some time to do some research I could have minimized my loss. I once heard someone say the only difference between a millionaire and someone who's daydreaming about becoming a millionaire is the way the millionaire uses their time; this is not the case for all millionaires but certainly represents a good percentage of self-made millionaires. We all have the same 24 hours in a day to get things done. How we use our 24 hours varies widely whereas some elect to migrate towards instant gratification as opposed to delaying the gratification and making some immediate sacrifices with the intent to be rewarded later in life. The Stanford marshmallow experiment led by psychologist Walter Mischel, then a professor at Stanford University, clearly demonstrated that kids who delayed rewards tended to have better outcomes than kids who took rewards immediately as demonstrated by their SAT scores, academic accomplishments, body mass index (BMI), and other life measurements. (Source: Wikipedia)

Develop good habits that will take you on a journey, not an overnight success. Build good habits early, so they will create success later in life, just like Mo Farah, who had developed the mindset and good habits that allowed him to overcome a major obstacle and win the gold medal. The bottom line is, the state and quality of life you achieve will have a high correlation to the habits you possess.

5

SETTING GOALS

A dream written down with a date becomes a goal.
A goal broken down into steps becomes a plan.
A plan backed by action makes your dream come true.
Unknown

There is an infinite amount of different ways to set goals and accomplish them. There are milestones and goals, but the process to achieve both will yield similar paths leading to success. Your vision and ability to see yourself as being successful is imperative. If you are unable to see yourself as successful it becomes very difficult for anyone else to see you as becoming successful. If you can visualize it, you can achieve it. Try shooting free throws with your eyes closed; chances are you will not make very many. Now if you open your eyes and begin shooting free throws, there is good chance you may make a few. Your vision allows you to focus on your target and goals with an increased level of accuracy. Eventually your vision will settle in your subconscious, begin to slowly move towards your conscious, and ultimately get you closer to your goals. Once you have visualized your goals, it's time to write them down. This is a very important process and it is often skipped. Writing down your goals may seem trivial at first but writing goals down will help you remember things that are important to you. As a college student when I took notes in class, I would remember more of the important material and consequently score higher on my exams as opposed to when not taking notes and recalling less of what was lectured on and consequently not performing well on the exams. Writing goals down makes you more efficient when it comes to recalling what needs to be done and why.

When I was 16, I subconsciously made a decision that I wanted a house with a white picket fence, and I knew that, at the time, there were only two ways I was going to be able to obtain it: selling marijuana at the park known as Lake Merritt in Oakland, which I was pretty good at, or going to college, a long shot for me because of a lack of education and mentorship. One night on my three-mile walk home after a night class at Oakland high school, I stood on the corner of Park Boulevard and MacArthur in Oakland, California, contemplating what to do with my life. In nearly 30 seconds of rationalizations and standing in the cold, it occurred to me that one option had a shorter life span than the other. In this short time frame I could clearly visualize a home with a white picket fence or being in prison for selling marijuana, which wasn't legal at the time. This stark contrast between going to jail and home ownership would ultimately influence the direction of my life and send me on a journey I would treasure for a lifetime. So, at that moment, I decided to believe in the power of "I can." Allow me to pause here and specify that I use the word "I" lightly and conspicuously, because in reality it was God who made all things possible for me, and still does. Be careful of what content you put behind "I can" because if you say "I can" or "I cannot," chances are they are both going to be right. Hence, if you are the editor of "I can" make sure the pronoun is positive and moving you towards your goals.

The image of a house with a white picket fence, and my belief in my own ability to obtain it, propelled me through many—and my most difficult—times in life, including going to college to obtain a formal education (BS in aeronautical engineering, master's in engineering, and a MBA), which allowed me to purchase multiple homes for residence—in excess of $1.7 million—and use my own broker's license to handle the transaction. This is why I say it's imperative to have a clear vision of what you want in order to achieve success. Even if you cannot figure out the details or how to take the next step, you must still dream big and emulate aspects of your dreams, which will keep you motivated, and you will see details fall into place.

Do not be caught up in the microscopic details, or you risk losing sight of the bigger picture, which could hinder your success. Always remember that, the bigger the goal, the harder the grind and the greater the reward. If you want and expect things to be easy, close this book now. Easy goals don't exist. A goal requires effort and sacrifice. There's no venture worth participating in that doesn't require some level of effort or struggle. Decades from now, when you're on your deathbed, you will not remember the days that were easy; you'll cherish the moments when you rose above your difficulties and conquered epic-sized goals. One of my goals in life was to run in a marathon, but I could always come up with many excuses why not to. Eventually, I gave in and ran in the run Disney 2018 Marathon, which required a lot of small successes, accomplishments, and achievements in order to get it done. You have unique matter in your DNA that allows you to achieve your goals. So, don't do what's easy; rather, maximize your utilities and astound yourself with your own greatness.

Timestamp your goals; this will hold you accountable if an activity is not completed within a specific date and time. This way, you can also go back and see if your goals were achieved or if they need to be modified. Most goals and/or projects come with a start and/or completion date. In your quest of being successful you should aim for completing your goals on time or ahead of time; this will help keep you being motivated to achieving your next goals. Football players go into a huddle to discuss their goals and plan to achieve their objectives while bringing clarity to their mission. Just because you are busy doesn't mean you are moving closer to your goals; moving horizontally when the goal is to advance forward keeps you busy but in the wrong way.

Sometimes when we are writing down our to-do list or goals and objectives we may start with the simple tasks that bring enjoyment, and when you look at your list of goals you will sometimes find the hardest of them all on the very bottom of the list. A good technique to address this phenomenon is to take your to-do list and turn it upside down, and start with the new first task, which was at the bottom of your original to-do list, synonymous to doing the hardest things first.

Another secret to staying motivated while achieving your goals is to tell 10 people about your goal(s). Sharing your goals with others may allow them to provide additional support or allow the haters to come out. There are apps you can link into a community that may be actively pursuing your same goals and allow you to become a card-carrying member of that community.

You will have many goals and they may change slightly as life progresses. One of my goals, after making it big in the dot-com Silicon Valley area, was to own a retail shoe store and capacity in a manufacturing plant to manufacture my branded goods. I was blessed with a retail store next to a Nordstrom department store. I was able to accomplish this after many years of selling women's shoes and apparel to pay for college. However, I was not able to secure private labeling/branding and manufacturing capacity. Be proud of your accomplishments, no matter of the magnitude or meagerness.

6

THE IMPORTANCE OF READING 20 MINUTES A DAY

Any book that helps a child to form a habit of reading, to make reading one of his deep and continuing needs, is good for him.
Maya Angelou

Start reading, continue reading, and accelerate your reading. Don't worry, it gets easier. Someone once asked Bill Gates: is there one super-power you'd like to possess? Bill Gates replied: the ability to read more. To me, that was very profound. He already reads 50 books a year. My desire to read came from reading Curious George's books when I was in the first and second grades. I did not graduate from high school, nor middle school, but upon graduating from college with a couple master's degrees, I felt I was burnt out on reading. What a huge mistake! After graduating from college I should have continued reading but I fell out of practice and conformed to society norms by renting a room, getting a job, and saving money to buy a house. Reading was not in the equa-tion after college, until one day I realized the advantage that I once had by reading hundreds of books while in college was slowly dissipating along with my value to the company. So I began buying books and read-ing again to add value. I learned how to build a data warehouse business by reading books and position myself for my next opportunity with a dot-com business, which offered me tons of stock options, a signing bonus, and a huge starting salary all because I took the time to research and build a business plan on how to implement a data warehouse. In the process of attacking your goals, whether it's a large salary, an office by the window, or spending quality time with your family, it will inevitably require you to continue reading even if you feel you are at your capacity of reading. The concept of stop reading is not an option; what you read becomes the option and the medium that can determine your destiny.

If you decide to stop reading and depend on third-party information (TV, podcast, Twitter, Facebook, Snapchat, Instagram, and radio), be aware that you will not tap into your full potential, which may have a direct impact on your lifestyle. Knowledge is power and one of the quickest ways to become knowledgeable, or an expert on a particular topic, is to read anything related to your field of interest. According to a study by the Pew Research Center, Americans read an average of 12 books per year using different types of mediums, not just hardback and/or paperback books. If you read 24 books a year, which is about one book every two weeks, you are reading 50% more than the average American. Remember, no one is going to give you a handout, especially when there are books on how to make $1 million with your eyes closed written by someone blind.

In our busy lifestyles, our attention is diverted in multiple directions, so we often find ourselves multitasking. For example, you might be working on a project, chatting on the phone, keeping an eye on all of your social media applications like Twitter, Facebook, Snapchat, LinkedIn, and Instagram to make sure nothing pops up and listening to a Pandora radio station. All this mini multitasking is diverting your attention into multiple area and not committing your undivided attention to one task, which could lead to stress and/or low productivity due to poor time management depending on the individual and the complexity of the task. Reading a book at least 20 minutes a day can increase your ability to focus and increase your vocabulary, and you will be amazed at your ability to engage in multiple topics and share information you have acquired in your readings.

7.

QUALITY TIME WITH GOD

Ask and it will be given to you; search, and you will find it; knock and the
door will be open for you.
Jesus

I advise you to be alone in a quiet place, away from any distraction, such as your phone, computer, and television, and seek God's word. Removing yourself from the typical distractions will allow you to focus on a message or sign God may be sending your way. Sometimes when I am driving and I'm distracted I miss my exit signs or street signs, which are supposed to be navigating me in the right direction. You don't want to miss any signs that are intended for you from God, which can mean the difference between being broke or rich, happy or sad. God is the antidote to loneliness, and even if you're not lonely and with friends or family He can enhance the ambience and your state of mind. You can use a symbolic gesture such as closing your right hand, as if you were grabbing the Lord's hand. This gesture will help you feel connected to Jesus and His presence in your life. We often see high-profile athletes when they do something spectacular they make a gesture to thank and/or praise God for their accomplishments. Whenever you feel lonely or happy or are facing struggles, reach out to the Lord, He already knows how you feel anyway. Spend time enjoying the Lord's presence, knowing how safe it is and you are not vulnerable. Seek the Lord's perspective on your life, because there are no do-overs; it also helps release your problems to a higher power, because He is continuously watching over us. "The Lord upholds all those who fall and lifts up all who are bowed down." Psalm 145:14.

8

HOW TO INVEST IN YOURSELF DAILY

Invest in yourself first. Expect nothing from no one and be willing to work for everything.
Tony Gaskins

How to invest in yourself daily is an ongoing process, as well as one of my favorite topics. There's a book titled Make Your Bed, written by Admiral William H. McRaven, who discusses how small wins add up to big successes. Success is generally paid for in advance through practice, repetition, patience, or preparation, all the hard work done before obtaining success.

Here are a few ideas you should practice overriding natural tendencies, which are not favorable to your body, mind, and soul. Dedicate resources to yourself; we spend an enormous amount of time helping and/or being judgmental about others when we should be allocating time, energy, and attention towards enhancing ourselves. If you don't invest in yourself, no one else will. Here is a list of self-enhancements you should participate in, which will be self-beneficial while being a resource for the common good:

1. Exercise. Exercise can improve your health and reduce the chances of developing diseases such as type 2 diabetes, cancer, and heart-related diseases.

2. Learn a new language. Society is becoming more diverse so learning a new language will help you communicate locally and abroad. I learned Japanese in college, which led to a job at Hitachi, a Japanese-owned company. Also, learning a new language improves your cognitive skills, memory, and listening skills.

3. Take a social media class. Communicating to the critical mass is generally done via a social media application such as Twitter, Facebook, Snapchat, Instagram, and LinkedIn. In fact I found my last three jobs via social media applications. The percentage of people who use some sort of social media has continuously grown: 2014-66%, 2015-70%, 2016-77%, and 2017-80%.

4. Go to a conference. Going to a conference will allow you the opportunity to network, develop your social skills, and learn from others; after all, how we learned to walk was by watching and/or learning from others. Also, conferences have the ability to excite you and motivate you towards your goals.

5. Join an organization. Joining an organization gives you a feeling of camaraderie; you can also develop new friendships that may land you that next great opportunity. Some organizations you can just have fun. I joined a golf club for the networking and to have fun.

6. Be a mentor. Being a mentor provides you the opportunity to help someone and reciprocity always comes into play. One of my dad's slogans is "each one teach one."

7. Create a vision wall. Write your goals down and hang them somewhere where you can see them daily, on your wall at home or in your office. I have my goals written down on my bathroom mirror, which helps me stay focused and sometimes provides that little extra motivation. If you write your goals down and put them in a drawer, chances are you might lose

sight of them; out of sight, out of mind. Creating a dream board with pictures of your rewards for achieving your goals can work as well.

8. Create a space that will inspire you. My inspirational space is in my home office downstairs away from distraction. I also get inspired to be super productive in libraries. Find out what works for you. Starbucks or sitting outdoors may work for you; we are all inspired in many different ways. The key is to be in the right place at the right time in order to allow your mind to work for you.

9. Hire a public speaking coach. This is especially helpful if you're aspiring to become a motivational speaker, keynote speaker, or leader; you will need to have good communication skills in order to be successful. Some would say it's not the public speaking we fear; after all we do this every day. It's the public embarrassment that gives us anxiety and nervousness.

10. Travel. Traveling helps to understand and appreciate the differences in individuals, cultures, religions, and races. Traveling also provides an opportunity for you to disconnect from your daily routines and to relax, have peace of mind, and be appreciative of what you have. When I was traveling abroad I realized just how poor others were and began to be even more grateful for the opportunities I had back at home. As the saying goes, "we never know what we have until we lose it."

9.

KNOW YOUR WHY

The two most important days in your life are the day you were born and the day you find out why.
Mark Twain

The day you were born and the reason you were born occurred simultaneously. The reason we are born is sometimes not very clear. It's confusing to some because our purpose in life varies widely. Some believe we are here to help others, while others may believe we are here to live a happy, full life. We all have unique values we can contribute to society, unique DNA that makes us different from the next person, and unique reasons why we believe we are here on earth.

Identifying your purpose and why you are here can be a tedious process, as some try to follow in their parents' footsteps, others may try to be the opposite of their parents, while others may take a self-assessment test, which is what I did while in college to help me figure what I was good at with the least amount of effort to maximize my utilities. Identifying your purpose and why you are here is challenging enough but applying yourself in the area of your purpose can be extremely rewarding. You are here for a reason, you are reading this book for a reason, and the world would not be the same without you. I recently discovered my "why"; it was subliminally in my consciousness for several years. I could not identify how to obtain it because of the numerous life obstacles and, like many others, I continued through life gaining different skill sets, certificates, and licenses to add value to myself, which allowed me to pay rent and eventually save up enough money to buy a house. Sometimes you may even feel great about what you are doing on a daily basis but in reality you could be moving further away from your goals and objectives.

I wasn't able to recognize or activate my "why," but activities supporting it kept coming to me, such as opportunities to motivate and share my experience with high school students while in college. Colleagues, pastors, and friends kept saying I innately had the skill sets to become a motivational speaker. Motivational speaking at the time seem reserved for only the very best speakers such as Tony Robbins, Eric Thomas, and others who had either incredible stories to share and/or ways to inspire individuals to take action. I have a picture of me speaking to a classroom of students sharing my experience and obstacles I had to overcome while achieving two master's degrees from Cal Poly SLO. When looking at this picture the teacher had the date written on the chalkboard behind me along with some notes she was sharing with students: the date read 1-26-1994. At that moment while sharing my story I knew what my calling to life was, which was to share with others how they too can achieve their dreams. My only setback was I thought there was more to becoming a motivational speaker and being successful at it had to be a lot tougher than what I was doing because it came so naturally and fluidly. So, I kept searching and hoping someone would tap me on the shoulder, reveal my skills to me, and then lead me to my "why." This is a great way to waste time, and this path is littered with corpses waiting for someone to breathe life into their "why."

Sometimes, you have to listen to the voice in your head that's telling you what to do, what's morally right, and not wait for confirmation from somebody else. I have a picture of me inspiring and motivating high school students during my last year at Cal Poly San Luis Obispo, while obtaining an aeronautical engineering degree, a master's in engineering, and an MBA. You might be thinking, "Oh, that's pretty average," especially in 1994, for an African-American kid. What makes this prophetic is I did not graduate from high school nor middle school, but developed an inspiration to motivate others although I had no one inspiring me to make it through school or life. One of the reasons I didn't graduate high school is pretty simple: I didn't graduate from middle school or junior high. And the reason I didn't graduate from middle school and junior high was because I was either in a foster home, group home, incarcerated at 150th Avenue in Oakland, California, in a boy's detention center, or living on the streets. I cannot remember a single day I came home from middle school or junior high school and did homework; I was nowhere to be found in the high school yearbook. When you are living in a transitional environment moving from place to place there is very little time to develop a routine are even have a vision; it's more about survival and that becomes your basic instinct. If you want something bad enough, you'll find a way to figure it out and get it done.

Fast-forward 25 years, I'm doing exactly what my passion is, which is to share with students and professionals some keys to being successful, inspired, and motivated in their careers and in school. However, getting to this point was not a straight line, but the most important lesson I learned along the way is to never give up on yourself because if you don't believe in your own dreams first, nobody else will. Usually, a person goes to elementary school, middle school, high school, college, and finally applies for and lands a job. However, my path was a very squiggly line and nothing close to the usual way life happens, as described above.

10.

BEATING THE ODDS

I am too positive to be doubtful. Too optimistic to be fearful.
And too determined to be defeated.
Unknown

Having the belief you can accomplish a particular objective even when the odds are stacked against you is the first step in beating the odds. There are many lottery winners who have won millions of dollars knowing the odds of winning a national lottery jackpot is approximately one in 14 million but yet millions of people continue to believe they have what it takes to be the next winner. One of many reasons they pursue the idea of trying to be the next vanquisher is because there is usually a big payoff of some sort if you are successful with your pursuit of conquering the odds. Many travel to Las Vegas in pursuit of beating the house odds but many leave Las Vegas unhappy at their attempts, because the odds are stacked against them. If you are going to make an attempt at being a champion, here is a list of suggestions to take into consideration:

A) Understand the risk versus reward. Oftentimes people are terrible at assessing risk because of the way they view the rewards as more desirable and thereby minimizing the risk associated with the rewards. In pursuing my formal education at Cal Poly the odds were stacked against me for a couple of primary reasons: 1) I chose an engineering major that required a lot of science and math background, which I didn't have, and 2) I had to work every week in order to support myself, which took time away from studying. I witnessed numerous students either leaving Cal Poly on their own or being expelled from the aeronautical engineering department because of academic reasons, and some chose to change majors. When speaking to some of the students leaving the engineering department and changing majors they said it was because they had underestimated the amount of work associated with obtaining an engineering degree and didn't want to continue risking being expelled from Cal Poly.

For me I felt as if my back was up against the wall and I had to risk it all, because I refused to go back home without a degree, which I knew would provide me with a better lifestyle than my friends without a degree. Discipline was and still is imperative to beating the odds; without discipline it will be virtually impossible beating the odds through hard work. Of course, some get lucky but luck equals preparation plus opportunities, which requires some level of discipline.

B) What are you passionate about? Knowing what you are passionate about will help you tap into your innate strengths and attributes, which are internally unique to you. Some may say you are better at achieving a certain goal based on what they see externally, but if you are not passionate about it chances are you will not succeed at your highest level or worse yet you may get harmed mentally and/or physically. People cannot see your heart beating from the outside; only you know what makes your heart beat with excitement internally. When you follow your passion you have the ability to provide seamless performances in a specific activity and utilize your innate ability, which will improve your performance, which is synonymous to having a superpower.

Here are some major types of strengths to help you determine your passion:

- Character (your mental and moral traits distinctive to you will drive your emotional state of mind and keep you on a motivational path to success)
- Intelligence (the ability to acquire and apply knowledge; some can acquire knowledge easily and quickly but lack the fortitude and ability to apply it)
- Interests (the state of being curious and wanting to learn; if you lack the interest in your goals it will begin to show in your results)
- Resources (have a deployable strategy in adverse circumstances; as mentioned, adversity is unavoidable if you plan on beating the odds without being lucky)

Understanding why you are committed to a particular cause will help you stay motivated and in the zone. Understanding your why will require work (why am I committing these resources for this event?) and have opposing forces, so make sure your why is strong and at the front part of your consciousness daily and share it with 10 people. The 10 people you share goals with will ultimately help you be accountable to your objectives. Some of the 10 people will question your validity for grinding it out as you are pursuing your goals because they may believe the odds are against you. Have a list of five reasons why you are committed to a particular goal; it will serve as reminders and help you stay on track.

Most of life's battles will be fought on the battlefield of your mind, so make sure you have a strong foundation, connection, and understanding of your why or you will be asking yourself why you are putting yourself through such misery during those challenging moments when doubt starts to creep in and odds seemingly are against you. Without a clear understanding of your purpose you will simply be tempted to abandon your goals at the first sign of discomfort. Do remember if you plan on beating the odds, never give up; it may take you a little longer but the mission will get accomplished.

11

SMALL WINS COUNT

Every strike brings me closer to the next home run.
Babe Ruth

Why do small wins count? If you are playing basketball then each made basket is an incremental step towards the ultimate goal, which could be winning the national championship. If you are working on a business plan each milestone executed correctly gets you motivated and closer to your end goal. Then the question arises, why isn't everyone creating small wins daily? The short answer is small wins require the ability to focus and some level of effort; the volume of both will vary between individuals and their tasks. I start my day with small wins, which builds up the momentum to tackle the larger wins in life. Every day as part of my morning routine I make my bed. By making my bed I have completed one of many small tasks that will need to be completed during my day. I once had to live in a shelter for homeless boys (St. Vincent de Paul) and every morning we had to make our beds and stand at attention until the nuns would come by and inspect the beds for completeness; after inspections we were off to start our day and rewarded with breakfast. So not only making your bed in the morning builds momentum but it will put you on a reward system, which gets you ready for the next task to complete with our neurons receiving and passing positive messages to our brain.

Small wins do count and they don't have to be perfect, although oftentimes I want my bed to be perfectly made. My son when playing competitive basketball wants his shots to be perfect; he has learned it's okay to aim for perfection but don't let it hold you back from taking the shot. There is a metaphor that says you can get paralysis through analysis, which is getting nothing done by overthinking your objective, whether it's developing a web page, starting a business, achieving your personal best, or taking that winning shot during the game. Realize that the ideal of perfection is not achievable because only God is perfect. Trying to be perfect can and will only hold you back.

There's a famous quote by Jim Lovell: "There are people who make things happen, there are people who watch things happen, and there are people who wonder what happened. To be successful, you need to be a person who makes things happen." Which one do you want to be?

Every small win counts and every defeat can be counted as a win too; it's a matter of perspective. By creating wins you know things went according to plan, but when you are defeated you should walk away with a lesson learned and use your defeat as a platform to stand on to create your next win.

In fact, long-distance running simulates life because you have to take a bunch of small steps to run 10 miles or even one mile. You can't take one giant leap and run 10 miles; it requires many small steps, time, resources, and energy. It's not about just buying a new pair of sneakers; it's about lacing them up, hitting the gym, and logging the miles until you reach your desired goal.

Here's the deal: figure out your goal, aim for it daily, be patient, persistent, and the rewards will come. As they say, when the student is ready the teacher will appear. Do not be afraid to take a risk; some people may say, "oh that's too risky" but consider the price tag of not being risky; besides, life is so risky no one gets out alive. Make sure you are taking some risks, you are learning from them, and you're creating small wins daily by focusing and applying your efforts. Do not be the batter with the bat glued to their shoulder afraid to take a swing because they may not hit the ball; swing, tear the cover off the ball, and hit it out the park for a home run and win the game of life.

12.

HAVE A PURPOSE

Allow your passion to become your purpose, and it will one day become your profession.
Unknown

You need to have a purpose and/or goal that is larger than the moment; for example if you're training to run a marathon you may have to run 5-mile, 10-mile, and 15-mile training runs on different days to prepare you for your 26.2-mile marathon run. The shorter runs will drive your subconscious and motivate you to continue running, because they serve a purpose of a favorable outcome such as a confidence builder. If you are planning on competing in sports, breaking a new record, obtaining additional credentials, starting a new business, or making a sales presentation, make sure you are doing things that are in alignment to your goals and serve a purpose to assist you with achieving your desirable end results. You do not want to build a bridge to nowhere or do things just to go through the motions without a purpose. On the flip side, your purpose should be like your mind actively connecting dots to generate an image of success before you physically connect the dots and experience success. For example, if you are preparing for a presentation, visualize yourself delivering the presentation. If you are anticipating making game-winning shots, visualize yourself making the shot. Your brain only needs two connections and it will figure out the third.

Most successful people will be out of bed by 5 a.m. because of the amount of activity required to be successful and live a normal life; your commitment to your purpose will demand you to rise earlier than most as your lifestyle will be different than most people's. The greater the goal, the more you need to be more efficient with your time. By prioritizing goals daily you will be reacting consciously to your subconscious in a favorable manner and holding yourself accountable to your purpose. You need to be able to count on yourself for continuous improvements, so make sure you are either adding value to yourself or someone else, otherwise your time spent here on Earth will not be spent wisely. When you create a sense of urgency you get things done. Your sense of urgency will set a new standard and continue to add value to yourself. Be sure you have an attitude to become biased for action and you will feel good about yourself daily as you are accomplishing tasks and moving towards your goals, while creating a cascading effect allowing other positive attractions and vibes to freely flow within your reach and increasing your self-esteem, discipline, and purpose in life.

13.

PREPARATION

*There are no secrets to success. It is the result of preparation, hard work,
and learning from failure.*
Colin Powell

Preparation seems like a simple and friendly concept, but the truth is
we often overlook it and, as a result, we end up being underprepared.
Without preparation, it's as if we were going into a battle when your
enemy has a machine gun and you have a water gun: inadequate preparation will yield you a loss or an uphill battle the majority of the time.
Should you opt to take 10% of your time preparing for your day, it will
make the other 90% predictable and enjoyable and lead to successful
outcomes. While preparing to run in my first marathon in January
of 2018, it required an enormous amount of preparation: everything
from meal planning and allocating times to run a variety of training
methods to accomplish the desired distance and speed. We often fail
to realize that completed tasks, conquered goals, and fulfilled dreams
come with an upfront price tag, which we pay with our time and resources. Success is paid for in full in advance. LeBron James, one of
the league's most accomplished and successful basketball players to
ever play the game, according to a 2016 report, indicates he spends
$1.5 million per year on his body.

ESPN's Brian Windhorst recently reported "James' annual body care costs in the seven figures." We witness many athletes getting injured due to inadequate preparation. Some weight lifters, when preparing to compete and lift heavy weights, take a creatin supplement in advance to increase their energy and endurance. The individuals are asked to front load, meaning take four times the normal dosage upfront and then use a much smaller dosage to maintain their levels to keep them in the target zone area. Runners, including myself, spend more energy getting started on the run and a lot less energy once we are in the zone.

You should preplan what you can the night before you go to bed, so you don't spend time thinking about those things in the morning. In theory, we should be preparing ourselves for moving on in life from preschool to first grade, from middle school to high school, and so on. It all requires some level of preparation to advance in life and the degree of preparation will determine your degree of success. God will not give you more than you can handle, so continue to prepare yourself to be in a position to handle and receive more. Oftentimes, we hear of people winning millions in lottery money and becoming homeless in just a few short years after winning the lottery, simply because they were not prepared to act or invest wisely. My dad would always advocate, if you fail to prepare you are preparing to fail. Prepare yourself through seminars, webinars, classes, networking, obtaining additional certifications, and licenses. This will allow you to be prepared, knowledgeable, and soon, an expert in your field. Sometimes, fortunes are made by just showing up prepared.

14

TAKE ACTION TODAY, BE REMEMBERED TOMORROW

Achievement seems to be connected with action. Successful men and women keep moving. They make mistakes, but they don't quit.
Conrad Hilton

Don't make rejections, failures, setbacks, or even successes of yesterday your focal point of today. You must believe you can move from yesterday in the quest of achieving your goals tomorrow. These are my mottoes:

1) Never give up.

2) Believe you can achieve anything through Christ.

As an avid snowboarder, one of the first lessons I learned in navigating a snowboard was to set my sight and vision on where I wanted to go and not where I was. You cannot dwell on the past while you are continually moving into the future because the present expires quickly. It's essential to set your sights on the future and things ahead of you, or it could be very catastrophic consequences. Most people heard or remember the death of Sonny Bono when he hit a tree while skiing. I'm not sure what caused the terrible accident. A lesson I learned from the incident is that it is vitally important to look into the horizon and make subtle changes when you are off course and not moving in the intended direction.

It's imperative you have a daily to-do list to keep you moving in the right direction and stay on course. You may need a partner to evaluate your progress periodically and provide feedback to help identify any weaknesses and strengths. If you would like to write a book, for example, you should take action today because the book is not going to write itself. There should be something on your daily to-do list associated with writing your book; it could vary from content creation to design and marketing. Sometimes, essential things do not make the to-do list because we are afraid to try something new. You don't have to know where all the pieces to a puzzle go in order to start the puzzle, but you should know it can be put together over time; it's a process. It can be hard to recognize the elephant in the room when you are standing too close to it. If you don't believe in your own greatness, it is probable you will never attempt to do anything great and allow your weaknesses to shine more than your greatness.

As a child, I used to swing blindfolded at a piñata hanging from a tree until I hit it and all the candy fell out. I was confident and determined that, at some point, I'd be rewarded for my efforts, which kept me swinging even when I missed the target. Unfortunately, we sometimes let our failures, missed opportunities, and opinions dictate our moves and rob us of our greatness. Be vigilant and careful of negativity and opinionated information from those close to you. If someone says you can't accomplish something you may start to attract reasons why you can't. For instance, if a child is taught they do not possess a particular talent to be successful, then there is a high probability the child will be a product of what they were taught. Hence, not all feedback is good or applicable to you. For me, I was in the third grade rehearsing for a talent show I wanted to participate in at school, when my stepmother said, "boy, you can't sing." I took her word but it was far from the truth. As a young person you have the tendency to go with what older people close to you say. Do not let others take something off your list of possible achievements you would like to accomplish just because they don't believe in you. Take action and move forward if you feel something is your calling. The road to success is always under construction; it's never smooth sailing and there will always be people doubting your abilities.

Your calling, goals, or objectives will require detail planning. Do you plan your days? Did you wake up today knowing exactly what you want to accomplish? If not, it's time for a change. One year from now, you will wish you had managed your time properly today to achieve your goals tomorrow. Remember: you will be loved for one generation, remembered by the second generation, and forgotten by the third generation. You want to do things that are significant so that people will remember you for those things you accomplished because they were epic. Take action now and envision an epic goal to share with 10 people.

Planning doesn't have to be some tedious and elaborate process. Just write down your objectives, review them daily and, if you find yourself drifting away, simply review your plan and adjust your activities accordingly. In preparing for my first marathon, many people were questioning me and asking what my purpose for running the marathon was. At some point, I had to question myself to ensure I was running this race for the right reason because the commitment of time, energy, and resources was significant. My running partner ended up in the emergency room the week before our race. My response to my doubters was simple: oftentimes, the gift God has provided us is seen through the recipient's vision and not through other people's vision. My objective was to run in a marathon because it was on my bucket list. I created a plan, reviewed it daily, made adjustments as needed, and got it done, and yes, you do hit a wall after running 21 miles, but guess what? I had a plan for that too.

At times, we literally do not know ourselves to be any better than what some opinionated, narrow-minded person may have told us, and we've acted on it and believed it to be true. Of course, this doesn't mean we are not good enough; it just means the other person could not realize our true talents. Do not let anyone distort your ability to reach your full potential; be sure to take action today and be remembered tomorrow, by exceeding your expectations.

15

SELF-TALK AND YOUR RETICULAR ACTIVATION SYSTEM

I figured that if I said it enough, I would convince the world that I really was the greatest.
Muhammad Ali

Self-talk is something most of us have experienced in some capacity. When you are consciously aware of negative self-talk, you can override it with positive self-talk or redirect the negative self-talk. In the book Positive Intelligence, Shirzad Chamine talks about why the majority of people's minds are acting as a sabotage 25% or more of the time. There are things you can do to decrease this sabotage percentage and increase the percentage of the time your mind is serving you. You cannot stop birds from flying over your head but you can redirect and prevent them from landing on your head and the same with negative self-talk. You would never walk up to a stranger and start criticizing them; hence, don't be so hard on yourself when the little voices in your head begin to echo negative vibes when things don't go as planned.

Part of the reason we become conscious of the self-talk, positive or negative, is because our reticular activation system (RAS), which is responsible for all of our senses except our smell, comes into play. RAS is essentially our brain's gatekeeper with responsibility for regulating our consciousness, and allows us to participate in everyday social cognitive behavioral responses to the outside world, ranging from sleeping to eating to having sex. So here is how it works: because of the 100 pieces of information our consciousness is aware of at any given moment it does not process all the information and our RAS acts as a filter and addresses the unique and sensitive information. For example, if you are in a crowded room with everyone talking, it appears to be all garbled background noise; once someone mentions your name your RAS springs into action and flags it to your consciousness; now you become aware that something is going on regarding you and you are ready to take action. Another common example is when you purchase a particular color car your RAS will act as a radar and begin to notice more of the type of vehicle and color you purchased. I bought a silver Toyota Camry for my son and suddenly I begin to notice the same car and color everywhere. Prior to purchasing the silver Toyota Camry I would not have been aware of one if it was parked next to me.

If you tell yourself you are afraid to fly, your RAS will zero in on all negative news flashes regarding airline accidents to reaffirm your self-talk and not the millions of safe flights that occur daily. Be careful of the information you and others are telling yourself. What you feed your mind will manifest itself as part of your character and moral qualities.

Your mind is unique in the sense that if you do not tell it a story it will create one for you; therefore, if you are going to be the author of the story, make sure it's a positive one. Be vigilant and focused on the positive in your mind and do not create negative stories that simply do not exist; this will also help you stay focused. Self-talk is something you should incorporate throughout your day. In fact, I have many conversations with myself and God throughout the course of the day thanking Him for all the things He has done for me. Gratitude is a great way to feed your mind, and generate positive self-talk at the beginning and end of your day.

16

POSITIVE SELF-TALK

You can't live a positive life with a negative mind.
Julette Millien

Speaking positively about yourself and/or someone else will yield positive results more times than speaking negatively about yourself and others. Affirmation statements are positive thoughts that are intended to inspire you to accomplish individual achievements. While in the medical sales industry I remember going into an account where they had told me and many other sales representatives, no, they were not interested in the products. I decided to fly down to LA to the account without an appointment with the intent to close the deal. I had told myself the decision maker is going to be there, the doctors and management team are going to love and endorse my product, and I would walk away closing one of the largest deals for the company. And as you can imagine, yes, I closed the deal, which allowed me be to win the trophy as star salesperson of the year. What you say to yourself positive or negative has the potential to become true. For example, if I would have talked myself out of going to LA because of the probability of the decisions makers not being there, I would have never been awarded for my efforts.

Positive self-talk is something you should incorporate in your thought process the moment you wake up; spending 10 seconds of silence in bed to smile and be grateful is always a good way to start the day. Self-talk is the internal conversation you have that could be short or long but the objective is to present your mind with positive thoughts, which will turn into positive actions towards a desired outcome.

If your thoughts are generally good, there is a possibility you're an optimistic person. If you're someone who harbors negative thoughts, such as I can never achieve that, this life is too tough for me, and maybe next time, there is a good possibility you are a pessimistic person . Some of Gulliver's Travels glum famous quotes were "We'll never make it and it will never work" and most of the time he was right. Practice just the opposite, such as we will make it and it will work, and watch your level of success start to escalate. There are also health benefits to positive thinking.

Researchers are continuing to explore the effects of positive thinking and optimism on health. Health benefits that positive thinking can provide are:

- Increased life span
- Higher quality of life
- Lower rates of depression
- Lower levels of stress
- Higher resistance to the common diseases
- Better psychological well-being
- Better cardiovascular health and reduced risk of death from cardiovascular disease
- Better ability to handle hardships and times of stress

It's unclear why people who engage in positive thinking experience these health benefits. One theory is that having a positive outlook enables you to cope better with stressful situations, which reduces the harmful health effects of stress on your body. It's also thought that positive and optimistic people tend to live healthier lifestyles; they get more physically active, follow a healthier diet, and don't smoke or drink alcohol in excess. Oftentimes throughout your day, quiet yourself and allow God's voice to be a beacon and heard, because His words are going to be positive in spite of the internal or external circumstances.

STOP TELLING YOURSELF THE WRONG STORY AND MOVE FORWARD

Don't be a victim of negative self-talk. Remember, you are listening.
Unknown

Most of us like stories of some sort; some like fiction, some like non-fiction, sometimes we find ourselves as part of a story. Why do we like stories? One of many reasons we enjoy stories is because there is usually something we can identify with, or something we don't identify with, a lesson learned, or we're looking to be inspired and motivated by a story. Some of our traditions, culture, and rituals have been passed down through storytelling, which helps us understand why something may have occurred and allows us to connect with a particular event on an emotional level.

Most of us have experienced moments when we thought someone was looking at us or following us and reacted, only to find out that person was thinking about something other than ourselves. Do not try and guess what others are thinking about you and then plot your reactions because oftentimes you will end up with two distorted views of reality, the first being your narrative of what an individual is thinking and the second would be your reaction to what you thought someone was thinking. Sometimes we are living in fear and insecurity, which may trigger an unnecessary reaction. An example is when I pull my car up to a red light and stop, sometimes I used to think the persons adjacent to my car at the light were looking at me, which used to trigger a level of insecurity and I would react by driving off fast or slow to separate myself from the individuals next to me. When I began to stop and see if people were actually looking at me, I found oftentimes the people adjacent to my car were not paying attention to me, so the stories I was feeding my mind were distorted and often did not warrant my reactions. When telling yourself a story it doesn't have to be everyone is out to get you; if you are going to be the narrator in your story, make it a good one. Try and create positive stories about and around you, especially if you are the main character in your story. By creating positive stories in your mind, this will minimize negative reactions, which oftentimes are not warranted. Sometimes we have to tell ourselves a story such as I'm going to go to the gym to run four miles because it will help me lose five pounds in five weeks. Sometimes your mind will try and divert your actions by saying you have other responsibilities, which will prevent you from moving forward to the gym. Sometimes we have to tell ourselves a story because if we don't our minds will create an unfavorable one for us. I've heard of the #5secondRule, which means if you come up with a thought and you need to take positive action count backwards 5-4-3-2-1 and physically take action or your brain will stop or interfere with you from creating the action required to execute. If you don't take action on your thoughts within five seconds there's a high probability you will not act in a favorable manner.

When talking to yourself in the morning, deciding on whether to go to the gym, you have about five seconds before an unfavorable outcome will happen. I also have a 10-second rule, which means if stories or conversations are not going in a positive direction within 10 seconds I try and minimize the negativity in the conversation and highlight the positivity or excuse myself from the conversation completely.

You should be jealous of your first 20 minutes of your day and make sure you are telling yourself good healthy stories, which will illuminate your morning and align yourself with your daily and future goals. You have to stop holding on to things that are not real. Let go of what was never really there; your intuition knows what I'm referring to. The pictures in your head and the stories you are telling yourself go against and directly oppose the present reality. Remind yourself that not everything is meant to be, not everyone is out to harm you. You have to seriously sit down with yourself and come to grips with facts and admit you were wrong about it all along. It was just an illusion that never really was what you thought it was. It's one of the most difficult realizations, which is to accept and realize that you feel a sense of loss, even though you never really had what you thought you had in the first place. Athletes encounter this problem quite often as they're practicing and they have a tendency to think the world is watching them when in reality the world is conducting the world's business. Stay focused on the business at hand, achieve some of your highest goals, be motivated enough towards your objectives and not distracted by illusionary pictures, activities, and stories that do not exist. The key is knowing this, learning from it, letting go, and moving forward.

18

REWARDING YOURSELF

When you're thankful for what you have, you are always rewarded with more. Try to stay positive and things will get better.
lessonslearnedinlife.com

Rewarding yourself is a tool to stay motivated and in the zone if applied correctly. You should reward yourself daily but only according to the size of your success. What I mean is you would not reward yourself with a Bentley for waking up early or on time but you should acknowledge the activity. Your rewards do not need to be lavish but they should resonate with you and make you feel good. If you're not a gym fanatic then being rewarded with a gym day pass is more like a punishment. The reward should be something you usually do not have time to do or don't allow yourself to do. Your brain will start linking success with positive energy. Reward systems convert potential energy to kinetic energy, driving you towards success. The list of ways to reward yourself is endless and depends on the magnitude of your success. Below is a list of ways to reward yourself:

- Help someone else
- Spend time with a loved one
- Go shopping

- Take a vacation
- Go skiing or snowboarding
- Play a round of golf
- Read a good book and catch up with friends
- Buy a new pair of running shoes or boots
- Go to a nice restaurant or discover new places
- Enroll in an interesting online course
- Go to the beach, stand up paddle boarding
- Take a day off and have a movie marathon
- Cook a big meal, pray, and celebrate with others
- Buy or lease a car
- Go to a concert

You can sometimes determine the success of the reward based on the aftereffects. What if you reward a 16-year-old by buying them a brand-new Porsche because they passed a math class and the 16-year-old later the same day goes out drinking and gets into a deadly car accident? The reward can be deemed ineffective for the occasion based on the results. Rewards are an important part of getting motivated but you should make sure rewards are appropriate for the occasion.

19

THE IMPORTANCE OF TEAMWORK

The best teams have chemistry. They communicate with each other and they sacrifice personal glory for the common goal.
Dave DeBusschere

When becoming motivated to accomplish a goal, it's extremely helpful to have a partner. Proverbs 27:17 in New International Version says: "As iron sharpens iron, so one person sharpens another." A good partner will hold you accountable even when he or she is not physically present. Your partner is the one who will support you when you are being challenged with achieving your goals and likewise you should be there to support your partner when they are needing support.

Psychological support is critical to the mental toughness you need to stay motivated daily, approaching your fluidity zone with your activities and getting through your to-do list.

I have owned a number of different businesses, anything from a mail-ordering business, data warehousing business, women's retail shoe store, day trader, medical distribution, and a real estate business. With each of my businesses I have owned I did not achieve the level of success needed to succeed because of my inability to partner up with someone with the same integrity, same goals, and equal or better mental toughness for when times are lean. Sometimes, we think it's better if we do everything associated with our new business by ourselves; after all, it's our idea, right? What I have learned after opening and closing many businesses is that it's better to use 1% of 100 people's time than 100% of yours because you only have 24 hours in a day. Partnering up reminds me of Bill the triathlete. Bill had decided to participate in the triathlon in San Francisco. However, he had failed to partner up and when he became overwhelmed because of the thick fog that had descended upon the bay, he chose to quit the race. Once the fog lifted Bill realized he was only 30 feet from the finish line. If Bill had a partner, his partner would've encouraged and/or forced him to complete the last 30 feet of the race. Which is synonymous to running a marathon and completing the last mile of the race because the crowd is there to cheer the runners as their partners to the finish line regardless if you finish walking or running. You and your partner will work together and push each other to become better competitors by working that much harder. Oftentimes partners or trainers will push you harder than you will push yourself.

I was training for a half marathon without my workout partner and had not hydrated properly on a Wednesday morning leading up to my Sunday half marathon race in San Jose, California. I started my normal cardio routine on a treadmill in the gym; within 90 seconds I became lightheaded, with rapid cardio increase. It was hard to breathe and I started sweating profusely. I got off the treadmill, walked into the area where the basketball courts were, sat on the bench, and fainted within seconds, knocking out three of my front teeth on impact. I was trying to drink some water prior to passing out, but my cognitive skills were impaired by being dehydrated and so I collapsed. This episode occurred a week prior to another half marathon I was training for, but my partner was there to help me and prevent any injuries. The first time I fainted, I had nobody training with me. If I had been training with somebody, they could've saved me from the hard fall. I checked in with my doctor after I fainted and his recommendation was not to run the race, which was three days away. I took a day off after getting my teeth repaired and decided to run in the race; after all, I had trained for it and my mantra is to "Never give up." I ran at a slower pace the first four minutes to ensure proper cardio and a feeling of hydration. I ended up running my fastest half marathon ever.

20.

HAVE ENTHUSIASM

Enthusiasm is excitement with inspiration, motivation,
and a pinch of creativity.
Bo Bennett

Generally, the person who brings the most energy to a purpose and/or competition will win and will be in a position to help others accomplish their goals too. Enthusiasm is contagious and infectious; people like being around those who have good authentic enthusiasm. The enthusiasm I am referring to is internal and displayed through your natural organic character and not pretentious. Life has simple biological rules such as reciprocity, meaning what goes around comes around. So, if we are presenting ourselves with good enthusiasm and not a Debbie Downer attitude, people will be attracted to us and want to collaborate and work with us. It's synonymous to sending out a certain frequency and someone tuning in and following you, like the law of attraction.

In the beginning of 2012, things seemed to be going in the right direction for me after spending two years in the medical sales field with a tremendous amount of enthusiasm daily that led to recognitions, awards, and promotions. However, by mid-2012, I was laid off, and it forced me to downsize from a larger room I was renting to a smaller room in the same house. My personal belongings were put in storage and I was receiving calls from the storage facility threatening to auction off my personal belongings if I did not come up with the monthly payments. This was also the year my car was repossessed by my girlfriend. So, enthusiasm was not at an all-time high at the time. But there was one shining star, which was my 10-year-old son, and he was somehow continually doing very well in and out of school, while I was going through a divorce and sharing custody with his mother. Somehow, God kept us living in the same city, which made things a little easier to manage from getting him to school to homework and extracurricular activities.

If you stay positive through adversity, the right person will discover the enthusiasm you have and may overlook some of the skills you don't possess and place you in a position to thrive. So, from 2012 to 2014 I focused on self-reliance and self-belief, in spite of the odds and always placing God first. By 2014, my enthusiasm and hard work had paid off. I went from being a 1099 wage earner to obtaining my first regional sales position, including Alaska and Hawaii, with a generous budget with a medical diagnostic manufacturing company. I was blessed to receive this opportunity, not because of my skill set or my experience, but because of the enthusiasm I displayed in the interview. I went on to win awards and to be recognized at the company as one of the best organizers, presenters, and closers. Always bring some enthusiasm to the party, as it will always be welcomed.

21

KEY COMPONENTS FOR SUCCESS

Anyone who has achieved anything in life knows that challenges and
failures are necessary components for success.
Former First Lady Michelle Obama

Being successful requires a number of different factors and being motivated to move consistently towards a goal is the key factor as there are many challenges along the way. Without motivation, there is no desire and, consequently, nothing gets done. Most successful people start their day off early to help maintain a balance in their life by exercising, spending time with family, recreation, personal development, and spiritual enrichment. Doing too much or too little of any of these activities could tip the equilibrium in your life and create problems. Here are ten things successful people have in common:

1. They start their days early
2. They are competitive
3. They aim for a goal and complete it without excuses
4. They are life learners and students of life
5. They are curious
6. They have a vision and the ability to focus
7. They are good communicators

8. They are creative
9. They have gratitude
10. They exercise

Part of being successful is providing service to others, no matter how small or large. One of the many benefits of helping others is reciprocity, meaning the old adage "what goes around comes around." For me, it's an easy concept because I believe in God and, not only do I receive reciprocity, but other favorable things take place in my life, and I consider them invaluable. Here are 12 keys to success you can use to unlock your potential:

1. Take immediate and decisive action
2. Create and pursue smart goals
3. Work outside of your comfort zone
4. Work on being productive, not busy
5. Measure and track your progress
6. Don't waste time trying to make things perfect
7. Spend time with quality people
8. Maintain a positive outlook and learn from failures and mistakes
9. Keep it moving, minimize cold starts, or start over
10. Continue making small improvements
11. Keep it simple and make logical, informed decisions
12. Don't make decisions when you are hungry, tired, or angry

Don't try to apply all the things on the list of what successful people have in common and the top 12 keys to success simultaneously. The goal should be to implement a few at a time and allow them time to be part of your lifestyle to ignite your passion and not dampen your motivation by trying to make them all part of your lifestyle overnight. The list is not prioritized, and more than likely you're already implementing some of the ideas on the list.

22

SELF-RELIANCE

Don't depend too much on anyone in this world, because even your
shadow leaves you when you're in darkness.
Unknown

Take the time to truly discover who you are and the unique gifts you possess and be sure to share your gifts with the world. The world would not be the same without you and your gifts, but each of us have a limited amount of days to realize true self-respect, which comes from true self-reliance. Most of society is challenged with either choosing conformity or self-reliance. Conformity is easily adopted by human nature. Self-reliance, which is on the opposite side of the spectrum, is unknown and unpredictable. Most people choose to conform to social norms because the risk of backlash and public embarrassment is so high it becomes easier to conform to social norms.

Changes come from within individuals' thoughts and actions. From within one person's thought, a team begins to form, and then a theme is put forward to create a movement, but the movement came from self-reliance on a thought that was executed on. Exercising self-reliance is depending on yourself to get something done on your own. We all rely on ourselves to get something done, whether it's crossing a busy street or solving a problem. Becoming self-reliant gets easier over time with daily use, but we do not want to overuse it because we do need to tap into resources to accomplish larger tasks. We all exercise self-reliance to some degree, but we should use it as a platform for campaigns. I can, I will, and it's done. Through self-reliance, you become stronger every day because nobody is going to be there daily telling you how great you are; you have to be there for yourself.

Self-reliance will also take you places you would have never explored. I was in seventh grade, sleeping in trucks, and traveling with a carnival, hitchhiking from Berkeley to Florida. While most 13-year-old kids were enrolled in middle school, I was too busy either hitchhiking or working at the circus, where my job was to set up and tear down the roller coaster. My co-worker Rex and I took many risks connecting tracks at very high altitudes, so I had to be confident in my abilities at a very young age. Here is what I learned: if you count on yourself daily, you will start and finish each day knowing you gave it your best; it may not be your personal best but you will finish and finish better than most.

I knew that through self-reliance I would eventually find my self-worth and not always confirm to social norms. I am not advocating alienation, isolation, or seclusion from others because we all need each other. You have heard this quote before: "if you want to get it done right, you have to do it yourself." This is partially right but it's much better to work with additional resources than using all of your own time. I am happy with the person I am today because I am able to rely on my self-reliance as part of my lifestyle.

23

SELF-CONFIDENCE

Self-confidence is the most attractive quality a person can have.
How can anyone see how great you are if you can't see it yourself?
Unknown

Self-confidence is required in order to achieve your goals. I have watched my son play competitive basketball for 11 years and after he misses a shot there is a high probability he will make the next one, because he has practiced shooting for thousands of hours. You have to believe you can achieve what it is you are trying to accomplish. This occurs through repetition; you also have to trust in your abilities and trust comes from being confident. The person who believes he can or cannot accomplish their goals is usually right on both occasions. You will always miss 100% of the shots you don't take; each seized opportunity motivates you to continue, but you can't move to the next level and be successful if you are not confident.

Always believe in your ability to accomplish your tasks no matter how big or small, remembering large tasks are comprised of smaller ones, so it may take a little longer but be patient and trust the process. You will succeed and become more efficient and confident on the next project, because success breeds confidence.

Each success becomes a building block and platform to stand on and to be in a position to see and be blessed with additional opportunities. These small wins will help catapult perception into reality. Self-confident people perceive themselves with the abilities to achieve their goals, which creates good opportunities; they go after their passion without compromising lifestyle and have happiness in their lives continuously. Here are a few things you can do to create or enhance your self-confidence:

1. Surround yourself with positive people. Make sure the people on your team are positive as well. Eagles fly with other eagles, not with chickens. You often can tell a person's destiny by the people they walk with.

2. Apply constructive criticism received from others, because sometimes we can't see our own faults that may be holding us back.

3. See yourself as the person you would like to be, and see yourself as others view you. Most people want to be around people that demonstrate high self-confidence. If you want to be a runner, then run; if you want be a singer, start singing; if you don't have the skills, then acquire them. Once you see yourself as the person you would like to be, others will recognize you as the portrayed individual.

4. Don't let setbacks hold you back. Life is not a straight path and often throws fastballs at which you swing and miss. Be persistent, never give up, and always bounce back from a setback and not be consumed; you will find a breakthrough. The fastballs life was once throwing you will become softballs and slow balls, which you will be hitting out of the park on a regular basis.

5. Write down 10 things people say you're good at or come easy to you. Select two of the things on the list you would like to work on, remembering a key component of self-confidence is building on small wins which quates to big success.

If you truly want to experience success, help others be successful by providing micro-level details on how they too can be successful. For example, if you are a successful businessperson and you know someone who wants to start a business, help them with a business plan and not just say good luck and stay motivated. If you want to help an athlete perform better then provide them with details on what they need to do to enhance their experience. Coaches oftentimes yell at their players to play better defense but never really show them what to do to put their bodies into a better defensive position. Provide detailed instructions to individuals and watch their self-confidence increase substantially as a result of self-empowerment.

24

TAKE RISKS

Taking chances is scary but there is something that should scare you far more than anything: missing out on something truly wonderful because you were scared.
Katherine Matheson

Living is about learning as you go, adding value to you and/or others while enjoying the process and the end results. Oftentimes there are levels of uncertainty that require different degrees of risk, some life-threatening and some life-changing. Most recently the world has been watching the rescue of 12 boys and their soccer coach trapped in a cave in Thailand on June 23, 2018. In a risky attempt to provide oxygen canisters to the trapped soccer team and their coach, a Thai elite navy diver lost consciousness and died. The dichotomy is living is risky business and, yes, you can lose a lot including your life, but the price tag for not taking risks is epic.

Life is so risky nobody gets out alive. Every thought, every interaction, every decision, every step, every time you get out of bed you take a small risk.

To truly be motivated daily is to know you are getting up and taking on that risk, and trusting yourself to overcome any risk in your path to achieve greatness. Get up daily with enthusiasm in pursuit of your goals. Whether it's financially related, project based, or looking for a new job, don't marginalize your life by rolling over in bed, closing your eyes, and thinking of a million reason why things can't be done; instead think of ways on how you can improve situations by tapping into your true talents. As the average person gets older, they become risk averse, meaning they minimize risk because of the perception of lost time if something goes wrong. It's harder to recover the older you get because you have less recovery time and quality working years. Studies have shown you will make your most money between the ages of 50-60. On the contrary, Mark Zuckerberg once told a group of young entrepreneurs at Y Combinator's Startup School in Palo Alto that it's risky not to take chances: "In a world that's changing really quickly, the only strategy that is guaranteed to fail is not taking risks." The greatest risk is not to take one; keep taking risks, life expectancy is too short not to.

25

INCREASING BRAIN CAPACITY

Minds are like parachutes—they only function when they are open.
Unknown

There is a notion or myth by American psychologist and author William James that the average person uses a small percentage of their mental capacity. Hence, the theory that the average person uses 10% of their brain capacity, while athletes receiving gold medals use 40%, and the people receiving silver and bronze medals are tapping into 20% of their brain capacity continues to grow in popularity. Here are some ways to increase your brain capacity regardless of what percentage you are currently tapping into:

1. Exercising can improve your cognition and memory, thereby increasing brain capacity.
2. Stay hydrated; your brain is made of approximately 80% water so a moderate decrease (2%) can reduce your concentration, vigilance, and performance.
3. Avoid an abundance of sugar, especially industrial, and trans fat in your diet; too much sugar can destroy neuron connections in the brain and decrease your ability to learn. Nuts,

blueberries, whole grains, avocados, and omega-3 fatty acids are all beneficial to your brain.

4. Neuroscientists have found that intermittent fasting improves neuroplasticity (the ability for the brain to change or adapt). Overfeeding your brain has a negative impact on diseases such as Alzheimer's and Parkinson's, while fasting decreases inflammation and increases cognitive functions.

5. Sleep is required to consolidate memory and learning. In short, if you don't get enough sleep you will have less brain capacity and not be making quality decisions.

6. Oxford scientists have discovered that while reading blood enters into the part of the brain that is responsible for your cogitation and increasing your ability to focus.

7. Minimize prolonged stress, which creates an atmosphere of decreased learning in the brain and can also lead to irritation, anxiety, and being distracted.

8. Get sunlight; higher levels of vitamin D in your system allows you to perform better and contributes to slowing down the aging process of your brain.

9. Meditation is known to reduce stress levels and prevent age-related disorders such as Alzheimer's or dementia.

When trying to increase your brain capacity try and use your different senses in ways you have not before. If you read, read about something you would have never read about; if your right hand is your dominant hand, try using your left hand for writing or brushing your teeth. Try smelling different types of seasonings and try to guess what they are. The list of ideas and utilizing your senses in different ways will increase your brain capacity. Try going home a different way today and when you arrive try closing your eyes and remembering where things are and how to get around.

26.

STAY FOCUSED

Life is like a camera. Focus on what's important and
you'll capture it perfectly.
Iron Tarsh

Part of being in the moment is the ability to focus and isolate yourself from temporary external activities that may create any distractions from your main objective. Your brain will reward you if you commit to focusing on your immediate objectives. You can use internal and external methods to help you stay focused. Your ability to stay focused will generate tons of success with most projects, tasks, or opportunities. The ability to focus and not to let your mind wander, especially under pressure, is priceless. Think about this: when the sun-rays, which are diffused and scattered around the planet, are focused through a magnifying glass, there's enough energy there to start a fire. If you stay focused on your goals, you can create the same energy and medium required to light a fire under your projects or goals.

There are a variety of ways to focus on major tasks and minimize concentration levels on minor distractions. You see a lot of athletes getting off buses and planes with headphones or earbuds on to focus on their game plan and minimize external distractions, such as news media and crowd noise. One reason these athletes are wearing headphones is they are guarding their thoughts and not allowing temporary or free residency on their brains by unauthorized users. Other techniques include relaxing and concentrating on your breathing (inhaling and exhaling) for 60 seconds, creating a do-not-disturb time zone, free from electronics. This will help quiet your mind and slow it down from wandering, since it's capable of processing a 100 thoughts per second.

A policy should be to avoid allowing others to take up free residency in your brain. Be jealous of the information you allow to enter into your mind to be acknowledged or processed. One of your goals should be to stay focused and maximize your zone time and not allow others to occupy your thoughts and time. When focusing, be SMART (Strategic, Measurable, Achievable, Reasonable & Teachable). Often, being smart will help bring clarity to life, goals, and ability to focus.

27

PRACTICE YOGA FOR BETTER SELF-AWARENESS

Yoga takes you into the present moment.
The only place where life exists.
Unknown

Practicing yoga is good for the mind, body, and soul for a number of different reasons ranging from detoxification, heart stimulation, developing strength, improving flexibility, breathing, focusing, and concentration. Yoga allows you to develop the mental focus that is required while you're in the zone, by allowing more oxygen to circulate to help manage your breathing, thereby helping you think more clearly.

While practicing yoga I had to be focused on multiple things such as controlling my muscles while going into my next pose, and my breathing patterns so I didn't get tired too quickly. Yoga is a big mental game that requires your undivided attention to maximize your focus. Therefore, you must stay focused while relaxing your mind simultaneously. Don't take this as an obstacle because like it or not, it is what you/we face daily, especially when we are driving in traffic.

One of the greatest benefits about practicing yoga is it allows you to be better connected with your inner self, present awareness, and focus. Yoga gives you the ability to be better connected to yourself, help you understand your limitations, and will allow you to have better insights into your life as you become more conscious in the way your body and mind work. Yoga can improve brainpower even more than conventional exercise. A study of participants performed significantly better after 20 minutes of yoga than after other forms of moderate to vigorous aerobic exercise done for the same time—vigorous being the proverbial word. So the next time you would like to increase your brainpower and flexibility simultaneously, grab a chair and do a yoga pose.

28

THE HEALTH GRID

Exercise is king. Nutrition is queen. Put them together and
you've got a kingdom.
Jack LaLanne (AKA the Godfather of Fitness)

Are successful people more fit, or are fit people more successful? That's almost asking if the chicken came before the egg. Being healthy and eating healthy requires a conscious mind initially, but over time your brain will adjust and your body will guide you on a healthy diet. There is some scientific evidence that says fitness may come before success.

Typically successful people are more motivated than individuals who are not. One of the reasons they are successful is they took an idea and moved it forward, where those who are not motivated sat back and may have had the same idea but said someone else has implemented it or will implement the idea in the future. Should that be the case the argument can be made that successful people's genetic makeup will drive them to move forward with a good fitness plan. The fact is, when people are physically active, their body goes into a fight or flight mode. This response releases an endorphin called Brain Derived Neurotropic Factor (BDNF), which gives you the ability to think clearly and better respond to business demands. When you exercise, you increase the amount of BDNF in your hippocampus, which is associated with the heightened cognitive functions, such as memory and emotion. For example, if you were to ask a successful person why they exercise and eat right, they probably would not give you the above answer. They, much like myself, just know you feel good afterwards, you have more energy after a great workout, your endurance levels are much higher, and more importantly you stay healthy longer.

In fact, when I was laid off, I had a substantial amount of hours banked because I had never taken a sick day and that's primarily because I was going to the gym and working out on a regular basis (five days a week), and it paid off in cash. So, you might be asking yourself now, if I get motivated to take action, can I improve my career success, my financial success, achieve my goals, better relationships, productivity, and self-awareness if I'm physically fit? Without question, you will improve in all those areas. Consequently, when you are fit, you will improve your mental sharpness and the ability to manage stress. Here are some household names that take their fitness seriously:

1. Michelle Obama: Wakes up at 4:30 a.m. every morning to get in at least an hour workout.
2. Mark Zuckerberg: "Doing anything well requires energy, and you just have a lot more energy when you're fit."
3. Oprah Winfrey: "I try and do something every day that allows me to feel active."
4. Richard Branson: "I seriously doubt I would have been as successful in my career (and happy in my personal life) if I hadn't placed importance on my health and fitness."
5. Mark Cuban: "I will find a way to get it done [a workout]. I think it reflects how relentless I can be in the business world as well."

The common theme among most successful people is they have realized to live a long and happy life, fitness is going to be a key ingredient to achieving that goal. The good news is there are a number of different ways to stay motivated to either get in shape or remain in shape.

29

WHY IS MOTIVATION LOST?

When you feel like quitting think about why you started.
Unknown

There are many reasons why an individual might suffer from low motivation, or lose it completely. Here are some of the most common ones:

1. **No fun:** Motivation is directly correlated to the pleasure received from participating. If there is no fun or excitement derived from the activity, motivation will be negatively affected.

2. **Fear of failure:** Motivation is to avoid a direct threat to self-worth. Motivation isn't lost, it's just going in the opposite direction. This creates an outward focus, rather than inward focus. You become tentative and don't work as hard, and as a result you have an excuse to fall back on (partying the night before a game). The performance is poor, and ability is not a question, just attributed to lack of sleep. If performance is good, then this just augments your ability in everyone's eyes; this is called a self-serving bias. If it's a good outcome, you attribute it to your efforts and abilities, and if the outcome is bad, you will just say it had to do with something external and beyond your control. At times, an individual will act like they

just don't care one way or another to protect themselves from getting hurt. They feel a nonchalant attitude will be a good cover-up. In reality, the only person they are trying to fool with this is themselves.

3. **Unmet needs:** Needs such as fun, improved skills, affiliation socialization, exchanging ideas, and competency. The most basic such as food, water, and safety must be met. The need for friendship and a sense of belonging to a social group are also very important. Then there are esteem needs, when individuals draw respect from others and are able to gain pride from their efforts. The last one is self-actualization: here lies the need to put forth the necessary effort to maximize the use of whatever innate talent individuals possess and develop a sense of who they are in the grand scheme of things. If these needs aren't being met, then motivation will diminish.

4. **Excess pressure:** If the perceived pressure is too overwhelming to perform, individuals will feel unable to handle it and they will just stop working towards what they are trying to accomplish.

5. **Sense of helplessness:** When people feel that, no matter what they do, it's either not good enough or won't make a difference so they say, "oh well, I can't do it so why bother trying" and give up. They feel they have no real control over the outcome and failure is inevitable, and this is why motivation is lost. For example, if a student is getting a D in biology and feels he really needs to buckle down to improve the grade, then studying harder becomes the solution. If the student studies day and night and really applies himself and still is getting a D, he may be less motivated to continue studying since he is still getting the same grade. The feeling is no matter what he or she does, they are going to get the same results. Hence, why put all this extra effort into something that he or she has no control over?!

6. **Plateau in performance:** When you reach the level of performance you've been striving for, you might back off a little. You become complacent with your performance, and that's when complacency becomes dangerous. Things change, people change, and you always have to be driving for a new and better way to improve upon things, including yourself. You don't want to become stagnant and have grass grow under your feet. If you keep doing what you've always done, you will yield the same results. You have to raise a new plateau and discover new territories. The way to help combat complacency is to continuously set new goals.

7. **Fear of success:** In this case, individuals are afraid of the perceived increased burden in regards to the expectation from others (more pressure, loss of privacy, and higher expectations). The fear of success can be seen by athletes who perform extremely well, but faltered just enough when it counts and under pressure and as a result are edged out by someone else.

30

STAYING MOTIVATED

If you are persistent, you will get it. If you are consistent,
you will keep it.
Unknown

Take it one day at time. You cannot rush the process without risking or compromising the moment. Theoretically, life is a long journey without instant success; only slow subtle changes in organic motivation. However, you can stay motivated by taking it one day at a time, enjoying the moment, and taking the pressure off of planning for the future. When you are able to be in the moment, organic motivation occurs, good things happen, and you're able to enjoy many more moments through your stimulation and motivation. If you are always thinking about the past or the future while in the moment, you will lack the focus required to stay motivated, because your thoughts are scattered.

Being motivated daily has no shortcuts, but starting each day early, frequently, and with gratitude, will serve as a foundation to supporting and staying motivated on a regular basis. Having positive rituals to include little successes before you leave for the gym or to work will have a significant impact on your day. Your daily rituals can be as small as making your bed and/or walking the dog before settling in and starting your day. One of the many reasons why it's important to start each day early is because you are getting a head start on 92% of the world by waking up at 5 a.m. or earlier, according to a national online survey conducted in January 2015 by Edison Research, while more than half the people in the survey are awake by 6:30 a.m.

According to CNBC Business News and Finance, Richard Branson told his company, in a blog post, that he gets up at 5 a.m. every day no matter where he is because it gives him a head start on the rest of the world. Apple CEO Tim Cook wakes up at 3:45 a.m. every morning to go through emails, exercise, and grab coffee before settling in to his workday. Oprah Winfrey usually wakes up between 6:02 a.m. and 6:20 a.m. and gets her day going by walking the dogs, followed by chai tea or a cappuccino, exercise, meditation, and breakfast.

We all have 24 hours in a day; most successful people are starting their day early for a good reason. There are studies that show that, even if you're not a morning person, willpower is highest in the morning, thus leading to better decision making and healthier choices, thereby adding positive energy to your day. Gratitude increases your physical and mental well-being, which in turn increases your motivation levels. Gratitude is an emotion we feel in response to receiving something good that is undeserved . Rituals motivate and move us. The act of rituals is a common thread that has linked humanity throughout the ages, regardless of ethnicity, culture, or religion. Unlike habits, which are often mindless, rituals are generally mindful and carrying out a series of actions for a specific purpose. Continue practicing positive rituals and you will increase your probability of staying motivated more often.

31

PRACTICE AND MOTIVATION

You have to work from one point to go to the other. So I admire work ethic, I think it should be reinforced through our neighborhoods, that everybody should work hard, practice makes perfect, you have to be dili-gent with what you want, you have to apply yourself, you have to motivate yourself. You have to do for self by yourself, and then you can do things for other people. That's what I had to do,
I had to do it for self.
Tupac Shakur

Motivation is a result for what you enjoy doing. Without passion, the desire to achieve optimal performance is difficult. To find and prac-tice your own motivation, ask yourself, "What do I want and how do I want it?" If you enjoy solitude, perhaps walking or running may be suitable. If you enjoy speed and quiet, then cycling would be a good choice. If you value working out with others, then team activities might excite you. To facilitate identifying your passion, answer the following questions:

1. What sport and profession would you choose if it were guar-anteed you would be somewhat successful? Looking at this from this perspective silences the self-critiquing that influ-

ences your life choices. Your answer is a reflection of what you love. If you are not involved in that sport, or profession, then ask yourself why not. Since you enjoy this activity, there is a good chance you will do very well at it if you try. Perhaps there is a good reason you are not involved in that activity. If so, what other activity offers you the same rewards and in alignment with your values? There are always multiple ways to achieve your goals. The key is to know where you are going, know what you love to do, and watch your path to your destination become illuminated.

2. What are five things you enjoy about your preferred activity? Your answers might include health, challenges, camaraderie, excitement, speed, sense of self-worth, opportunity for self-improvement, or just fun. List your values and apply yourself accordingly and you will inherently begin to rehearse motivational techniques by simply engaging in activity you love, thus gaining a better understanding as to why you love them.

32

GUIDES FOR MAINTAINING MOTIVATION

When nobody else celebrates you, learn to celebrate yourself. When no-body else compliments you, then compliment yourself. It's not up to other people to keep you encouraged. It's up to you. Encouragement should come from the inside.
Joel Osteen

Once you have discovered your passion, be vigilant that you are exercising some guidelines to ensure your motivation is firing even during adversity. Your level of motivation is directly proportional to the pleasure you receive from participation in your activity. Motivation and enthusiasm evaporate rapidly if there's no pleasure. Lack of interest and boredom are the greatest challenges in peak performances.

Make sure the fun factor is part of your guidelines, as it should include changing your routine up, giving yourself rewards, and including others in what you are trying to accomplish, whether you are a public speaker, athlete, professional, or executive in your profession. Excessive activity or practice is harmful when it causes burnout. Regardless of how passionate you are about what you are striving to achieve, establish moderation and incremental changes in your routine. Moderation fuels motivation over a period of time.

Constantly monitor your ego. If you measure your self-worth by the results of your activity, then your activity can become a very dangerous mechanism for ego deflation. Given a string of failures, you will begin to avoid those situations and your motivation will drop. Remember, failures are platforms to success and the opportunity to improve on results. Finally, keep your perspective. If you have a tendency to take yourself or others too seriously, then lighten up a little, have fun, and enjoy the moment. Tomorrow's a new day!

BEING IN THE ZONE

Hard work beats talent when talent fails to work hard.
Kevin Durant

Being in the zone is performing at your highest level. According to Wikipedia, "in positive psychology, flow, also known colloquially as being in the zone, is the mental state of operation in which a person performing an activity is fully immersed in a feeling of energized focus, full involvement, and enjoyment in the process of the activity."

Breaking down the zone can be characterized as when a runner gets to a point in the run where they feel like they are running effortlessly, enjoying the run and getting more energy as they continue their run. For me, when I run a nine-mile run, I usually get into my zone around the third mile. At mile three I'm focused on my run and have optimized my steps and breathing, allowing me to be completely realized, focused, and completely involved in what I'm doing.

Kobe Bryant once described being in the zone as having supreme confidence and the desired result will occur. Japanese call it "satori"— the magical state where a player is completely focused on the task at hand, relaxed and mentally clear (Albinson & Bull, 1990). Some common characteristics of being in the zone are:

1. **Relaxed:** Research has proven the best performances occur when you are slightly above your normal state of arousal; you are energized and relaxed, it's a subtle balance. This state of being can come and go in a moment's notice.

2. **Completely focused:** You are completely immersed in the moment and the only thing you're focusing on is what you are doing at that moment.

3. **Confident:** You should expect to be successful, not hope or wish. It's trusting your instincts and intuition to do the right thing; the catch is if you are prepared, you can be confident of a favorable outcome, as Kobe Bryan explains: he knows his shoot is going to be good, everything around him slows down because he has practiced shooting.

4. **Effortless:** Things just tend to happen for you with little or no effort. For that time and moment, you can accomplish great things with little effort; it could be giving a presentation or closing a deal.

5. **Automatic:** Things are just happening; if you're a basket-ball player your three-point shot is going in without protest and without consent; your target seems to get bigger and not smaller.

6. **Fun:** When you're in the zone, you are enjoying your activity so much that someone would be able to look at you in the eyes and see the excitement you are experiencing. When you're having fun, time seems to pass quickly, but certainly comes to a crawl when you're not having fun. If you are enjoying a book the pages are going to turn much quicker than reading a book that you have no interest in when it takes forever to finish it.

7. **In control:** You feel that, no matter what happens, you are in control; whatever you think to happen, it does. You have incredible control over your emotions and how they are perceived. When you are in control of your future and you feel this way, epic things are going happen.

Being in the zone is a state of mind we all can achieve by applying ourselves accordingly. If you want to reach your zone you should be involved in an activity that will challenge you and not be too easy of a challenge. If your challenge is too easy you might get bored and if it's too hard it won't be fun and you might just give up. When I run my nine miles on Sunday it's usually a good challenge for me but one I can complete and it allows me to enter in my zone around mile three because I'm completely relaxed, my heart rate is at good rhythm, and I'm enjoying the run.

If I was to choose to challenge myself to run 50 miles I might just give up because I would be overwhelmed; on the other hand if I chose to run one mile that would not be very challenging and chances are I would not reach my zone because the run was too easy. Hence, to reach your zone find an activity that's challenging but not too hard or easy and you will be able to reach your zone and receive benefits from all the elements associated with being in the zone. For me I feel great after my runs and I have accomplished something great at the beginning of the day.

In conclusion, there are many ways of getting into the zone depending on your activity, which can be writing a book, playing an instrument, or being involved in a sports activity. Therefore, the length of time required to reach your zone will vary. Getting to your zone has some very similar characteristics that we all have in common, which are rituals, the ability to focus, and motivation, whether it's internal or external motivation. You will also need some kind of goal when trying to get into your zone; for a golfer it could be continuously hitting great shots, for me it's my nine-mile run. After a while my body gets used to running nine miles so I have to add more distance or vary my run with inclines to keep it slightly challenging and not boring. While getting into our zone inevitably there will be some self-talk in our minds; hopefully it's positive or you can override any negative with a mantra. As the narrative to the self-talk you control what you say to yourself and how you react.

Lastly, have confidence because confidence exudes positive energy and positive energy is a component to motivation and with the right motivation you have untapped potential and the ability to be in the zone daily.

BIBLIOGRAPHY

I.   DJ Khalid with Mary H.K. Cho | KEYS, First Edition. New York: Crown Archetype Publishing, 2016

II.   Admiral William H. McRaven | MAKE YOUR BED, First Edition. New York: Grand Central Publishing Hachette Book Group, April 2017

III.   Jocko Willink | DISCIPLINE EQUALS FREEDOM FIELD MANUAL, First Edition. New York: St. Martin's Press, October 2017

IV.   Steve Chandler with Scott Richardson | 100 WAYS TO MOTIVATE OTHERS, Third Edition. New Jersey: The Career Press, Inc., 2012

V.   Shirzad Chamine | POSITIVE INTELLIGENCE, First Edition. Austin, Texas: Greenleaf Book Group Press, 2016

VI.   Karlene Sugarman | WINNING THE MENTAL WAY, First Edition. Burlingame, California: Step Up Publishing, 1999

VII.   Chugliang Al Huang | THINKING BODY, DANCING MIND, First Edition. New York: Bantam Books, 1992

VIII.   Jon Wertheim | THIS IS YOUR BRAIN ON SPORTS, First Edition. New York: Crown Archetype, 2016

IX.   H. Norman Wright | A BETTER WAY TO THINK, Spire edition. Grand Rapids, Michigan Baker Publishing Group, 2015

DO YOU HAVE 33 WAYS TO GET MOTIVATED & STAY IN THE ZONE?

Walter Patrick, MBA, is available to speak at schools, associations, organizations, and businesses. For information on these programs and seminars, and to inquire about Walter's schedule, please contact:

Walter Patrick, MBA
Waltp123@me.com or www.walterpatrickjr.com

Please send me _____ copies of 33 WAYS TO GET MOTIVATED & STAY IN THE ZONE, by Walter Patrick, MBA.

Please send cost of book + $3.00 shipping and handling ($2.00 for each additional book). Send check or money order, please see website for address.

Made in the USA
Las Vegas, NV
08 April 2022